The contents including but not limited to the accuracy of events, people, and places depicted; opinions expressed in this book are the rights of the author; permission to use previously published materials included; and any advice or actions advocated are solely the responsibility of the author, who assumes all liability for aid work and indemnifies the publisher against any claims stemming from publication of the work.

Copyright © 2023 by Deborah Watford Rox. All rights reserved.

No part of this book may be or transmitted or reproduced, downloaded, distributed, reverse engineered, or stored in or introduced into any information storage and retrieval system, in any form or by any means, including photocopying and recording, whether electronic or mechanical, now known or hereinafter invented without permission in writing from the publisher.

Sud10 Inspirations LLC
501 E. Oates #494805
Garland, TX 75049

ISBN: 9798853912748

Embrace Yourself for the Amazing Person You Are!

You are a child of the King, made fearfully and wonderfully. Remember to love and cherish yourself for the unique individual that you are.

Unmask Me

and you will see my true Identity

Sud10 Inspirations LLC
Publisher

Unmask me and you will see my true identity.

I don't mean these physical clothes you see.
I mean my beauty,

,my charisma and my style.

Sit down and let's chat awhile

and you'll discover that I am confident,

bold,

and smart.

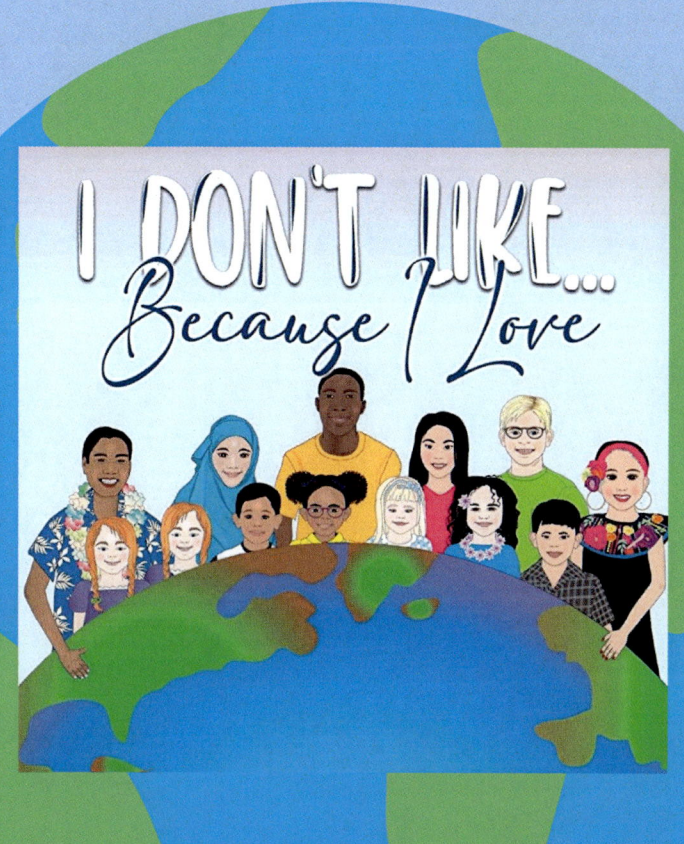

So don't let where I come from or my clothes offend you.

When you look at me,

I am worthy!

I am intelligent!

I am charismatic!

I am creative!

Broadening Your Lexicon

Here are three new words to enhance your vocabulary:

1. Charismatic: The ability to charm and influence others. (adjective) (p.24)

2. Charisma: The ability to win over others. (noun) (p.4)

3. Chat: To engage talk; conversation. (verb) (p.5)

Create a list of "I Am" statements to describe yourself.

- I am... _____
- I am... _____
- I am... _____
- I am... _____
- I am... _____

I am fearfully and wonderfully made to be a child of the King... Yes, that's me!

--Psalm 139:14

Made in the USA
Coppell, TX
04 October 2024